07/23   200

(g)

MOO

SALLY CLARK

Playwrights Canada Press
Toronto

MOO © Copyright 1984, Sally Clark
Playwrights Canada Press
54 Wolseley St., 2nd fl. Toronto, Ontario CANADA M5T 1A5
Tel: (416) 703-0201 Fax: (416) 703-0059
e-mail: orders@puc.ca   http://www.puc.ca

Playwrights Canada Press acknowledges the support of The Canada
Council for the Arts for our publishing programme
and the Ontario Arts Council.

Canadian Cataloguing in Publication Data:
Clark, Sally, 1953-
    Moo
A play
ISBN 0-88754-476-2
1. Title.
PS8555.L37197M66   1989   C812'.54   C89-094008-8
PR9199.2.C53M66   1989

Front cover photo by *Ed Ellis*
Cover design by *Tony Hamill*

Fourth Printing: October 2001. Printed and bound by AGMV Marquis,
Quebec.

This play is dedicated to
cads, rotters and bounders.

MOO

Moo received its world premiere at *NovaPlayRites '88*, Alberta Theatre Projects' annual Festival of New Plays, an Official Participant of the Olympic Arts Festival, Calgary. *Moo* was a co-production of Alberta Theatre Projects, Calgary and The Belfry Theatre, Victoria, with the following cast:

(in alphabetical order)

SARAH	*Pat Armstrong*
DOCTOR/CHARLIE/CLERK	*Ray Hunt*
MRS. MACDOWELL/NURSE/JANE/PATSY	*Susan Johnston*
MR. MACDOWELL/WALLY/DOUGALL	*Brian Linds*
DITTY MACDOWELL	*Jane Logie*
HARRY PARKER	*Weston McMillan*
MOO	*Wendy Noel*
MAUDE GORMLEY/SUSAN/NURSE	*Jan Wood*

Directed by Glynis Leyshon.
Set and lighting design by Warren Carrie.
Costume design by Pamela Lampkin.
Stage manager — Charlotte Green.

Moo was previously published in WHAT magazine.

Moo was produced at Factory Theatre in Toronto, January 1989 with the following cast:

(in alphabetical order)

DITTY MACDOWELL	*Robin Craig*
HARRY PARKER	*Richard Donat*
NURSE/MRS.	
MACDOWELL/PATSY/JANE	*Barbara Gordon*
MOO	*Patricia Hamilton*
MAUDE GORMLEY/SUSAN	*Brooke Johnson*
DOCTOR/CHARLES/HOTEL	
CLERK/ORDERLY	*Eric Keenleyside*
SARAH MACDOWELL	*Brenda Robins*
MR. MACDOWELL/	
WALLY/DOUGALL	*Michael Simpson*

Directed by Jackie Maxwell.
Set and lighting design by Terry Gunvordahl.
Original music score by Leslie Barber.
Costumes by Linda Muir.
Stage manager — Hilary Blackmore.

Running Time

Moo should run approximately 45 minutes for each act. With the exception of blackout after the first scene, the play should be performed without blackouts or fades.

Characters

This play can be performed by eight actors: 5 women and 3 men.

MOO

HARRY PARKER	*Moo's husband*
SARAH MACDOWELL	*Moo's oldest sister*
DITTY MACDOWELL	*Moo's sister*
MR. MACDOWELL	*Moo's father*
MRS. MACDOWELL	*Moo's mother*
MAUDE GORMLEY	*Harry's second wife*

NURSE/RECEPTIONIST

DOCTOR

DOUGALL	*Moo's son*
PATSY	*Harry's third wife*
CHARLIE	*Sarah's husband*
JANE	*Sarah's daughter*
SUSAN	*Jane's daughter*
WALLY	*Moo's boyfriend*

ORDERLY

Suggested Casting

Ditty
Harry
Moo
Doctor/Charlie/Hotel Clerk
Mr. MacDowell/Wally/Dougall/Orderly
Maude Gormley/Susan
Nurse/Mrs. MacDowell/Patsy/Jane
Sarah

Author's Preface

My grandmother used to tell me stories of women whose lives were ruined by anonymous evil men known as "rotters." Rotters seduced wealthy women and then deserted them, making them the butt of family consolation for years to come (a far more dire fate than the actual desertion).

According to family lore, one of my great aunts had the misfortune to fall in love with a rotter who, in the grand rotter tradition, ruined her life. I could never quite piece together the tragic image of the betrayed lover with my garrulous aunt who shocked and confronted everyone within range. I began to wonder about the rotter and whether in fact, when he seduced my great aunt, he got more than he bargained for.

I would like to thank the Ontario Arts Council and the Canada Council for their generous support.

I would especially like to thank Jackie Maxwell, Clarke Rogers, Patricia Hamilton and Sky Gilbert for all their help and encouragement.

Sally Clark

Act One, Scene One

A man, standing, is holding a gun. A woman enters, stops, stares at the man. The man raises the gun, points it at the woman and fires. Black.

Act One, Scene Two

Seattle, 1925. Insane asylum. Front desk.

HARRY

(to DOCTOR) As I've said, I've been worried about her. We've tried consultations with Dr. Swan and he and I both think she'd be better off here for a month or so on a trial basis.

MOO

(to RECEPTIONIST) We're visiting his sister. I've never met her. Harry's never wanted me to meet her. He thinks it would upset me.

DOCTOR

If you'll sign right here, Mr. Parker.

MOO

What are you signing, Harry? Is she coming out? She can't stay with us, Harry. *(to* RECEPTIONIST) She can't stay with us. I said I'd meet her but I don't want to bring her home with us.

HARRY

(laughs uneasily) Delusions.

MOO

Does she look like you, Harry? *(to* RECEPTIONIST) Isn't it a shame when people go like that?

DOCTOR

Come along, Miss Parker. I'm sure you'll feel right at home here in no time flat. *(guides her away)*

MOO

What are you doing? Harry, what's he doing?

HARRY   He's taking you away.

MOO   Aren't you coming? I don't want to meet her all by myself. What'll I say to her?

HARRY   Goodbye, Moo.

MOO   HARRY! (to DOCTOR) Stop grabbing me. *(rushes up to* HARRY) Harry! What's going on?

DOCTOR   .I was afraid this was going to be difficult. You should have prepared her.

HARRY   Moo, you're going to stay here for a while.

MOO   WHAT!

RECEPTIONIST   Now now, Miss Parker.

MOO   Mrs. Parker.

DOCTOR   Now, Mrs. Parker, we understand you need a little rest. You remember Dr. Swan?

MOO   Of course, I remember Dr. Swan.

DOCTOR   Did you like Dr. Swan?

MOO   He was all right, I guess. What's all this about?

DOCTOR   Dr. Swan has advised that you rest here for a short time and your brother has agreed.

MOO   My brother.

DOCTOR   Mr. Parker.

MOO   That's my husband. HARRY!

HARRY   Crazy.

MOO   HARRY WHAT THE HELL IS GOING
                   ON!

HARRY   Mad as a hatter.

MOO   HARRY!

HARRY   I've tried everything.

DOCTOR   Please Miss Parker, your brother feels that —

MOO   My brother is dead.

HARRY   There's no reasoning with her.

MOO   He's dead, goddammit. He was killed in
                   the war. Harry fought in the same
                   company with him.

DOCTOR   I see. Displacement personnae.

RECEPTIONIST   Quite.

DOCTOR   Now, Miss Parker, come along.

MOO   Harry. This isn't funny, Harry. Tell them
                   who you are.

HARRY   I'm afraid I can't do that, Moo. I am not
                   your husband. I am your brother.

MOO   Harry.

HARRY   I am your brother. Goodbye, Moo.

MOO   *(screams)* H-A-A-R-R-R-Y!!!!

Act One, Scene Three

HARRY *and* DOCTOR.

HARRY	She always had a vivid imagination. Of course, she liked me when we were young, but I wasn't always her favourite. I mean, she never expressly selected me as such. Not when we were young. No, that happened later. Much later. After George died. I suppose when George was killed, I was all she had left so she became dependent on me. And later, obsessed with me. Moo's a lot younger than George and me. Do you think that has any bearing on it? Her, being the youngest. The youngest are usually strange, aren't they? Sibling birth order. I remember reading something along those lines. It's just that, Doctor, may I be frank?
DOCTOR	Of course.
HARRY	I am sick to death of being her love object.
DOCTOR	Yes, I can see it would get tiresome.
HARRY	And now this whole business of our being married.
DOCTOR	She wears a wedding ring.
HARRY	She bought it herself.
DOCTOR	It's quite an expensive ring.
HARRY	She has good taste.

DOCTOR   She mentions sisters.

HARRY   Oh God, the sisters. I thought she'd forgotten about them.

DOCTOR   No. She's quite specific. She wants me to get in touch with them. She's quite insistent about it.

HARRY   The sisters. I'm trying to remember when they entered the picture. When she was very little, she had a friend who was the eldest of a whole family of sisters. Yes. That's right. But Moo hadn't started talking about sisters until just after George was called away. I was called shortly after so I'm not really familiar with that whole side of her madness. In fact, when I returned, I was willing to let the whole thing slide. I thought: so, she has a crush on me, so, she'll outgrow it, but it began to affect my life. I couldn't go anywhere without her calling me. Following me. And women! Out of the question. The minute she got wind of any female involvement, she'd call them up, badger them. That was when the husband business entered into it. *(pause)* Is there nothing we can do?

DOCTOR   Nothing. She is utterly convinced you are her husband.

HARRY   It's hopeless.

DOCTOR   Can you think of anything which might have triggered it?

HARRY   When she was nineteen, she was shot in the head.

DOCTOR   Aaaah.

Act One, Scene Four

MOO, *alone on stage.*

MOO   And he tried to kill me. He tried to gun me down. No. I'm not getting hysterical. Have you ever had someone try to gun you down. Well, it makes you think. This isn't a laughing matter. I don't know what you're laughing about. You're not laughing. Oh, sorry. I thought you were. I'm a little confused. But it's true. Dammit. It's true. He tried to kill me. Why? How should I know!

Act One, Scene Five

MOO *and* DOCTOR.

MOO	The first day, Harry came to our house to tell us the news about George —
DOCTOR	George.
MOO	My brother.
DOCTOR	You have another brother.
MOO	No. Just one. George.
DOCTOR	And are you married to George as well?
MOO	No. He's dead.
DOCTOR	Were you ever married to George?
MOO	He was my brother.
DOCTOR	But you are married to Harry.
MOO	Harry is not my brother. George is. But he's dead.
DOCTOR	I think we have a little problem here.
MOO	Look, Harry is lying, I don't know why he's lying but he's lying. Call my sisters.
DOCTOR	You have sisters?

MOO   Yes.

DOCTOR   How many sisters?

MOO   Two.

DOCTOR   Do you like your sisters?

MOO   Would you just call them, please?

DOCTOR   Do you like your sisters?

MOO   They're all right.

DOCTOR   Don't you like them?

MOO   I like them. But they drive me crazy. My whole family drives me crazy. Sorry. I didn't mean that. They don't drive me crazy. I just wanted to get away from them so I ran off with Harry.

DOCTOR   Don't you like your family?

MOO   Forget it.

           Pause.

DOCTOR   What possible motivation would Harry have for pretending to be your brother?

MOO   I don't know. I don't know why he signed me in here. I have no idea why —

DOCTOR   But, you, on the other hand, have any number of reasons for imagining Harry to be your husband.

MOO   What!

DOCTOR   Fear of men, dislike of women —

MOO   I want to go home!

DOCTOR   Now, don't get upset, Miss Parker.

MOO   MRS. PARKER. DAMMIT. MRS. PARKER, MRS. PARKER, MRS. PARKER!

DOCTOR   I see.

Act One, Scene Six

In a hospital room. MOO *is in a straitjacket, lounging about.*

HARRY *(enters, stares at her)* Don't you think you're carrying this thing a bit far?

MOO I thought I'd dress for the occasion.

HARRY You're overdoing it.

MOO Am I? Why don't you untie me, then.

HARRY *(unties her)* How did you get this thing? They don't usually put people in these.

MOO I've been very naughty. I didn't eat my vegetables.

HARRY There. It's undone.

MOO Are you sure?

HARRY Yes.

MOO *flings straps around* HARRY *and ties him to her.*

HARRY Hey!

MOO I'd just like to take a good look at my brother. It's been so long since I've seen him.

HARRY You don't have to be two inches from my face. *(tries to untie straps)*

MOO	*(giggles)* What's the matter, Harry? *(trips him)*

> *They fall on the floor.*

HARRY	Jesus! CHRIST! GET OFF ME, YOU BITCH!
MOO	My own sweet little brother. *(kicks him)*
HARRY	OW!
MOO	You goddamn prick! I'll kill you!! *(kicks him furiously)*
HARRY	NURSE!

Act One, Scene Seven

HARRY *and* MAUDE GORMLEY.

MAUDE   You're thinking of her again, aren't you?

HARRY   No. I'm not thinking about her.

MAUDE   Yes. You are. I can tell.

HARRY   Well — stop staring at me then. If you'd
                 stop watching for signs and just relax
                 maybe, we might be able to enjoy
                 ourselves.

MAUDE   We did before.

HARRY   You did.

MAUDE   You said you loved me.

HARRY   I did. I just don't like being watched.

MAUDE   Why can't you talk about her?

HARRY   There's nothing to say. She was crazy.

MAUDE   If she wasn't crazy, would you love her
                 still?

HARRY   Goddamn it, Maude, I'm with you, aren't
                 I? Isn't that enough for you. I've left her
                 and I'm with you.

MAUDE You only left her because she was crazy. If she was sane, you probably would have stayed.

HARRY How do you know I didn't drive her crazy?

MAUDE Did you?

HARRY No. I don't think so. I think she had a head start on me.

MAUDE Was she born crazy?

HARRY Who knows. I don't want to talk about it.

MAUDE What sort of things did she do? You know. Crazy things.

HARRY Maude, do we have to talk about her?

MAUDE I'm interested.

HARRY You're nosey.

MAUDE I want to know all about you.

HARRY You don't give a damn about me. You want to know all about her.

MAUDE I guess I do.

HARRY It's morbid.

MAUDE This is strange, Harry. I don't know how to say this exactly but —

HARRY But.

MAUDE   I liked you a lot better before.

HARRY   You did.

MAUDE   Yeah. And I've been thinking about it.
                   Maybe, when I was madly in love with
                   you, it's only because you were with her
                   and you had, like, "assumed" some of her
                   traits. People do that, don't they, Harry?

HARRY   What?

MAUDE   Take on the other person's character. So,
                   I loved you because you were living with
                   her and that must mean that I was actually
                   in love with the two of you. Or, oh
                   Harry, this is awful —

HARRY   What.

MAUDE   Or, maybe, I was actually in love with her.
                   Just her. Not you at all. Does that make
                   me a lesbian, Harry? Do you think I'm a
                   lesbian?

                          HARRY *gets up and walks backwards*
                          out of the room, staring at MAUDE
                          cautiously.

MAUDE   Harry?

Act One, Scene Eight

MOO, *in straitjacket.*

MOO   I suppose, these days, it's all in one's
        credibility. If you are short, you have less
        credibility than a tall person. If you are a
        woman, you have less credibility than a
        man. If you are short, a woman and
        wearing a straitjacket — well, forget it,
        you have no credibility at all. I go to the
        mirror and I stand and look at myself
        wearing this stupid get-up and I think —
        "Can I believe this woman?" And the
        answer is of course, "No." And I look
        and tell myself who I am, where I'm from
        and how I came to be here and the answer
        is again, "No." In theory, if I did have
        sisters and family, they should eventually
        start looking for me. I don't see anyone
        except Harry and then, only once a week.
        Harry, the man I love to hate. I look
        forward to his visits. For the week, I rage
        against him; I beat myself against padded
        walls. I plot and plan all the nasty things
        I'm going to say to him. Yet, when he
        shows up, I'm so bloody grateful it's
        ridiculous. I'm even starting to believe
        he's my brother. The thing I can't fathom
        is, if Harry isn't my brother, why is he
        doing this to me? That's what doesn't
        make sense. That's what makes me think I
        must be crazy. Then, it all clicks neatly
        into place. It all makes sense, then, I'm
        getting very tired again. I don't know
        whether it's drugs, bad food or just
        fatigue, but I sleep all day. I wake up for
        meals, read the odd book. But mainly I
        sleep. And await rescue.

Act One, Scene Nine

Vancouver, 1919. Grounds of the MacDowell house. MOO is shooting cans. She throws a can up in the air, shoots, hits it. Her sister, SARAH, walks up behind her.

MOO   Hello, Sarah.

SARAH   Getting out your frustrations?

MOO   At least I have an outlet.

SARAH   Why do you shoot?

MOO   Practice. I want to be good.

SARAH   Why, though?

MOO   Something to do.

SARAH   I worry about you, Moo.

MOO   Why? What's wrong with wanting to be good?

SARAH   Nothing. But this will never get you anywhere.

MOO   By anywhere, you mean marriage.

SARAH   No. I didn't mean that at all.

MOO   I tell you what, Sarah. I'll marry the first man who can outshoot me.

SARAH   I wasn't talking about marriage, Moo. I
               simply meant if you're going to be good
               at something, you should find an
               occupation. Shooting is useless.

MOO   I enjoy it.

SARAH   Since you're not going to get married, you
               should —

MOO   Who says I'm not going to get married.

SARAH   You did.

MOO   No, I didn't.

SARAH   It's hopeless trying to have a conversation
               with you. I don't know why I bother.

MOO   You look very nice, today. Charlie still
               lurking about?

SARAH   It's Charles. He doesn't lurk. And yes, he
               is coming by.

MOO   You're going to marry him, aren't you?

SARAH   Why do you dislike men?

MOO   I don't dislike men, Sarah. I simply dislike
               Charlie — sorry — Charles. If having an
               aversion to the little scum implies a general
               dislike of the male species, forgive me —
               Mea Culpa.

SARAH   Charles is going to be very successful.

MOO   Single-minded men usually are. He'd have
             to be successful. He doesn't have any
             choice. There isn't enough room in his
             brain to admit any other possibility.

SARAH   I don't know why you dislike him. What
             is wrong with Charles? Tell me that.

MOO   He's boring.

SARAH   Boring. What's boring?

MOO   Charlie is boring. Oh, you want me to be
             more specific. Charlie is boring because:
             one, he has no imagination; two, he likes
             cars — always distrust a man who likes
             cars; and three, he plays golf! Golf is a
             boring man's game.

SARAH   My God, you talk a lot of drivel.

MOO   They get the little matching hats and
             matching gloves with the knuckles cut out
             and the cute little shoes that match the
             gloves and the cute little clubs that have
             little hats to match the hat the golfer's
             wearing. And it's all cute as hell.

SARAH   Lots of interesting men play golf.

MOO   I'm sure that's possible. But interesting
             men don't look like two-toned Christmas
             trees.

SARAH   Charles loves me.

MOO   And that's why you're marrying him.
             When George gets back you'll see what a
             bore Charlie is.

SARAH	You don't understand, Moo. He's a good man and he adores me.
MOO	And that's enough.
SARAH	For me it is. I will love him in time. When a man adores you, he makes it impossible to do otherwise.
MOO	I think it could be a real nuisance after a while.
SARAH	Charles is restrained. He won't overdo it.
MOO	It's your life.
SARAH	Yes. It is. *(stalks off)*
	MOO *starts shooting. She throws a can up, shoots, hits it. Throws up another can, hits it.* HARRY *approaches and watches her.*
HARRY	Ah, excuse me.
MOO	*(sees him, stops shooting)* Who are you?
HARRY	Harry Parker. *(stretches out a hand)*
MOO	*(does not take it)* What are you doing here?
HARRY	I'm sorry to disturb you, but I'm looking for Mr. MacDowell.
MOO	An odd place to look, don't you think?
HARRY	I couldn't find the house.

MOO   The house is back there.

HARRY   You have a fair amount of ground.

MOO   Is my father expecting you?

HARRY   No. He isn't.

MOO   What business do you have?

HARRY   I'd rather not say, right now. I'd like to speak to him, personally.

MOO   He's in the house.

HARRY   Yes. Well. Pleased to meet you. *(waits for* MOO *to give her name)* Right. Well, I suppose I should go to the house. *(starts to head off, stops)* You were shooting just now.

MOO   Yes.

HARRY   I hate to ask you but can I have a go?

MOO   Ah...

HARRY   Just for a moment?

MOO   Oh. All right.

HARRY   You had a tin can around here.

MOO   You're very observant.

HARRY   *(finds it)* Something I used to do. You try and keep the can up in the air for as long as possible.

MOO   Pardon?

HARRY   You just keep hitting it so it stays up there.
                   *(throws the can up, shoots, keeps the can
                   up for a long time)*

                        MOO *stares, dumbfounded.* HARRY
                        stops, hands rifle back to her.

                   Thanks. I needed that. *(leaves)*

                        MOO *stares after him. She throws the
                        can up, tries to shoot it, misses. She
                        stares back after* HARRY.

Act One, Scene Ten

MacDowell living room. MR. *and* MRS. MACDOWELL, *their daughters:* SARAH, DOROTHY *and* MORAGH, *and* HARRY PARKER, *a visitor.*

MR. MACDOWELL	I am indebted to you, Mr., er —
HARRY	Parker.
MR. MACDOWELL	Parker. Quite. It slipped my mind. All the confusion.
HARRY	I understand, sir.
MRS. MACDOWELL	A glass of sherry, Mr. Parker?
HARRY	No, thank you, Ma'am.
MRS. MACDOWELL	You must.
HARRY	If you insist, thank you. *(takes glass)*
MRS. MACDOWELL	Did he know he was going to die?
HARRY	I think so, Ma'am.
MRS. MACDOWELL	Did he have a vision?

SARAH   Mother!

MRS.
MACDOWELL   I hope he had a vision. When I die, I
                    want to have one.

MOO   You have them all the time, anyway.

MRS.
MACDOWELL   You're a very selfish girl, Moragh. You
                    can't live for yourself, you know.

MOO   What does that have to do with it?

SARAH   Moo's just being funny, Mother.

MRS.
MACDOWELL   How can she make jokes at a time like
                    this. I don't believe she even cares.

SARAH   Mother, we have company.

MRS.
MACDOWELL   Quite. Excuse me, Mr. Parker. I often
                    have these tete-a-tetes with my girls.

MR.
MACDOWELL   Jesus, it's awful.

MRS.
MACDOWELL   What, dear?

GIRLS   What, Daddy?

MR.
MACDOWELL   Oh sorry, I was just thinking.

MRS.
MACDOWELL   It's going to be very sad without him.

MR.
MACDOWELL   It's going to be unbearable.

SARAH   Pardon, Daddy?

DITTY   Pardon, Daddy?

MR.
MACDOWELL   Bloody unbearable.

HARRY   I'm sorry, Mr. MacDowell. I don't know what to say.

MR.
MACDOWELL   There's nothing to say. Nothing to do. He was close to you, was he?

HARRY   Yes sir. I'd say so.

MR.
MACDOWELL   What are your plans, now? Going to see your family?

HARRY   Well — ah —

MR.
MACDOWELL   You're welcome to stay here, if you like.

HARRY   Oh now, Mr. MacDowell. I really couldn't inconvenience you. You don't even know me —

MR.
MACDOWELL   So, it's settled. You're staying here. Jean!

MRS.
MACDOWELL   Yes, dear.

MR. MACDOWELL	Mr. Parker is staying here.
MRS. MACDOWELL	That's nice, dear.
MR. MACDOWELL	We need another man in the place.
MRS. MACDOWELL	Yes, dear.
MR. MACDOWELL	Brighten things up.
MRS. MACDOWELL	Yes, dear.

Act One, Scene Eleven

MOO *and* HARRY. *1919.*

HARRY   Self deceit. That's what the cause of it all
               is.

MOO   The cause of what?

HARRY   Old age. Ill health. TB. Senility. Our
               bodies are designed for perfection. Our
               brain is meant to function logically. But
               because we are indoctrinated from birth
               with a particular brand of ethics, morality
               — all of them, utterly illogical — we are
               lost. The brain realizes this. But it tries to
               make sense out of it, anyway.
               Consequently, it jams, malfunctions, and
               twenty years later, the person dies of
               tuberculosis.

MOO   Just like that.

HARRY   Sometimes, it takes ten years, sometimes
               fifty, sometimes it happens overnight. The
               person just snaps.

MOO   So, one must always tell the truth.

HARRY   Only to oneself. You can lie as much as
               you like to other people.

MOO   Why would I want to lie to other people?

HARRY   Why not. You, Moragh, are a wallower in
               self-deceit. It will catch up to you.

MOO	Do you lie to people, Harry?
HARRY	Of course.
MOO	To me?
HARRY	To you more than anyone else.
MOO	Why?
HARRY	Because you're special. And because you need it.
MOO	You're an odd man.
HARRY	Yes. Convince yourself.
MOO	If you could do anything at all, what would you like to do?
HARRY	I'd like to live by myself on a desert island.
MOO	Don't you like people, Harry?
HARRY	Not particularly.
	Pause.
HARRY	You don't agree with me.
MOO	About what?
HARRY	Self-deceit.
MOO	I'll think about it.
HARRY	No. You won't.

Act One, Scene Twelve

MOO   I knew the moment I laid eyes on Harry
Parker that he was mine. I wanted him
and nothing was going to stop me from
getting him. The strange thing is, when I
think about it rationally, there wasn't
really much to want about Harry. He
wasn't particularly good-looking, although
people said he was; I didn't find him
handsome. But he had a certain look in
his eyes. A depth and a wildness. The
look of a man just slightly out of control.
And I knew I had to have that. When I
think about it, Harry wasn't even
particularly good company. He spoke
rarely but he always led you to believe that
he possessed information that went far
beyond what he said. And he was a good
shot. He was a very good shot.

Act One, Scene Thirteen

SARAH

I warned Moo about him. Right from the beginning. I said stick with the good men and you can't go wrong. But do you think she'd listen. She was determined to do it her way. That's the way she's been all her life. Everything had to be her way. And Harry — well, what can one say? He was insignificant, really, I mean, he ruined Moo's life but in the grand scheme of things, he was insignificant. Pity, she never saw it that way.

Act One, Scene Fourteen

DITTY   The only thing anyone will ever tell you about Harry Parker was that he was very handsome. That's all anyone really knew about him. I knew he was a rotter the moment I laid eyes on him. And of course, I stayed away from him. Couldn't stand the man. Can't say why. I just loathed him. That's all. *(pause)* And that's all I'll say on the subject. He was very handsome.

Act One, Scene Fifteen

> HARRY *is shooting.* MOO *stands at a*
> *distance, tossing tin cans in the air.*

DITTY   *(enters)* Hello, Harry.

HARRY   *(stops shooting)* Hello, Dorothy.

DITTY   I like it when you call me Dorothy.
You're the only one who does.

HARRY   It's a very nice name.

DITTY   Oh? Do you think so?

MOO   H-A-A-R-R-Y!

HARRY   Yes. I do.

MOO   H-A-A-A-R-R-Y!! Are you going to hit
the can or not?

HARRY   Just a minute, Moo.

DITTY   I wish I could learn to shoot.

HARRY   Didn't Moo ever teach you?

DITTY   Oh — no — she never had time.

HARRY   Well, it's quite simple.

DITTY   Oh, would you show me?

HARRY   Of course.

MOO   H-A-A-R-R-Y!

HARRY   I'll show you right now.

MOO   *(marches up to* HARRY *and* DITTY*)*
                 Harry, what do you think you're doing?
                 I'm waiting for you. Hello, Ditty.

HARRY   Dorothy wants to learn how to shoot.

MOO   Dorothy?

DITTY   Yes. Harry's going to teach me.

MOO   You never wanted to shoot before.

DITTY   Well, I do, now.

MOO   I'll bet.

DITTY   Harry, would you be good enough to show
                 me.

HARRY   Oh yeah. Well, you hold it like so,
                 (shows her then hands rifle to DITTY*)*

DITTY   *(picks it up)* Oooooh — it's heavy.

HARRY   We need a target. Moo, would you mind?

MOO   Mind what.

HARRY   Tossing some cans in the air.

MOO   She'll never hit those.

HARRY   I'll guide her the first time.

                 MOO *glares at him and walks off at a distance.*

DITTY   Thank you, Moo.

HARRY   *(behind* DITTY*)* Now, you hold the gun so.

                 HARRY *picks it up so he is behind her. Holding the shotgun, he places* DITTY'S *hand on it.*

DITTY   *(giggles)* Ooooh it's so heavy.

HARRY   You'll get used to it.

DITTY   Will I?

HARRY   And you — um — put your hand there. Now, don't pull the trigger.

DITTY   Trigger?

HARRY   Yeah, that thing there. Keep your hand steady. I'll keep my hand on yours. The gun has a recoil so be careful. Now, you look down the barrel.

DITTY   The barrel?

HARRY   Yeah — um — there's a little sight there — see it?

DITTY   Oh yes.

> HARRY *has his face pressed near*
> DITTY'S.

HARRY   Well, you use that to sight the target. So, you... ah — *(kisses her neck)*

DITTY   *(squeals)* Eeee!

> *The gun goes off.* HARRY *and*
> DITTY *are thrown backward. They sit*
> *up and look in the direction of* MOO.

DITTY   Moo? Moo? MOO! Oh my God, you've killed her!! MOOOO!

> DITTY *runs to* MOO, *whose head is*
> *bleeding copiously.*

Act One, Scene Sixteen

MOO *and* HARRY. MOO'S *head is bandaged.*

HARRY You don't think I tried to gun you down, do you, Moo?

MOO Of course not, Harry.

HARRY Your sister. She's mad, you know.

MOO Which one?

HARRY Right. They're both crazy.

MOO Are they?

HARRY I brought you something. How is your head?

MOO It's all right. You just grazed it.

HARRY Good.

Pause.

HARRY I'll probably have to leave soon.

MOO I guess you will.

HARRY I didn't do it, Moo. It just went off. That's all.

MOO I know. What did you bring me?

HARRY	Oh sorry. Here. *(hands her a package)*
MOO	*(opens it)* Perfume. Oh Harry, perfume. *(looks at it)* "My Sin." What sort of perfume is that?
HARRY	French.
MOO	I've never worn perfume before.
HARRY	Wear it now.
MOO	*(sniffs it)* It smells awful.
HARRY	*(sniffs it)* No, it doesn't. Smells like you. *(smells her neck)* Run off with me.
MOO	Elope?
HARRY	No. Run off.
MOO	Harry, you want to marry me?
HARRY	Have it your way. *(kisses her)*

Act One, Scene Seventeen

> HARRY *and* MOO'S *bedroom, 4:30*
> *a.m.* HARRY *tries to sneak into bed.*

MOO   *(in bed)* Where have you been?

HARRY   Oh, hi, dear.

MOO   *(sits up, turns on light)* Where have you been?

HARRY   Oh, out and about.

MOO   It's 4:30 in the morning.

HARRY   Is it that late? I had no idea —

MOO   Where were you, Harry?

HARRY   I was out.

MOO   But you go out all the time. You're out all day.

HARRY   Business.

MOO   You come home for dinner. Stay for a few hours, then, you're out again.

HARRY   I've got to get myself sorted out. I have to get started again. You'll just have to be patient.

MOO   You never had so much business, before.

HARRY
It fell through.

MOO
What sort of business do you do, anyway, Harry?

HARRY
It's too complicated, Moo. You wouldn't be interested.

MOO
I want to know.

HARRY
Look, Moo, I'm tired. Things aren't going too well for me and I don't really want to talk about it when I get home.

MOO
But I want to know.

HARRY
You'll just have to wait. I don't know myself what I'm doing.

MOO
Why do you have to hide things from me?

HARRY
I'm not hiding anything from you, I just don't want to talk about it.

MOO
What am I supposed to do while you're out all day?

HARRY
Do what most women do.

MOO
And what is that!

HARRY
How should I know. I'm not a woman. Other women stay home while their husbands do their business. Can't you be like most women? Ask me if I have a nice day at the office, kiss me on the cheek and leave it at that.

MOO   You don't have an office, Harry.

HARRY   How do you know that.

MOO   I've tried to find it, Harry.

HARRY   So now, you're spying on me.

MOO   I just want to know who I'm married to. I
               want to know what you do all day.

HARRY   You want to control me.

MOO   I don't want to control you. It's a simple
               question.

HARRY   I don't know what you do all day.

MOO   Do you want to know?

HARRY   Not particularly.

MOO   Harry, we're married.

HARRY   Yeah.

MOO   We're supposed to share things.

HARRY   Yeah.

MOO   We're supposed to talk to each other.

HARRY   I'm not a very talkative man, Moo. You
               knew that.

MOO   Couldn't you at least try?

HARRY	I'm trying to get my business sorted out and I just don't feel like talking about it. It's as simple as that. You don't have to make a goddamn issue out of it.
MOO	Where were you tonight?
HARRY	Jesus Christ! Give me some room. All I want is some room.
MOO	Harry, I love you.
HARRY	*(wearily)* I know that, Moo.
MOO	Do you love me?

Pause.

HARRY	Yes, Moo.
MOO	Say it, Harry. I need to hear you say it.
HARRY	I love you, Moo.
MOO	Do you mean it, Harry?
HARRY	*(no response)*
MOO	Do you mean it?

Act One, Scene Eighteen

MOO   They're right, of course. I should be in here. Not for the reasons they think but for the simple reason that I want to see Harry. Wanting to see Harry is a disease. Not yet categorized, but it is a disease. I have every reason in the world not to want to see Harry. He tried to gun me down. Oh yes, he tried to do it. He married me — abducted me, more to the point. He stole all my money and he put me in a loony bin. And I still want to see him. To scream at him? Hurl abuse at him? Get revenge? Oh probably — but mainly to see him. It's almost as though Harry and I, together, form this single magnificent organism. The only drawback being that Harry comes out on top and I wind up getting the shit kicked out of me. Maybe Harry does this to women. That's what I'm not sure about. If he does this to all women, then I'd be an even greater fool that I thought I was. There'd be nothing special in it. I'd simply be another one of his victims. In which case, I'd make a severe attempt to cure myself and forget about him. But I think he just does it to me. Harry has this compulsive desire to screw me around and I have this compulsive desire to be screwed. But not just by anyone. Any other Tom or Dick would not do. It has to be Harry.

Act One, Scene Nineteen

Hospital room.

NURSE	We have a surprise for you, Miss Parker.
MOO	Mrs. Parker.
NURSE	Yes, well, whatever.
MOO	Mrs. Parker. It's not whatever. It's Mrs. Parker.
NURSE	*(to door)* I don't think she should see you. Not after last time.
HARRY	*(enters)* Hello, Moo.

MOO *glares at him.*

HARRY	*(to* NURSE) It's all right. You don't need to stay. We'll be just fine.
NURSE	Are you sure?
HARRY	Yes.
NURSE	All right. I'll be outside if you need me. Just call. *(leaves)*
HARRY	Well, Moo, and how have you been?

MOO *glares at him.*

HARRY	Not too chatty today, are we?

MOO *continues to stare.*

HARRY   *(shifts uncomfortably)* Well, dear, the nurses tell me you seem to be much better.

MOO *removes slippers slowly, performs partial strip tease, removing her clothes piece by piece.*

HARRY   *(pretends not to notice)* Of course, they did say you have bouts of depression. Now, are you unhappy, today? You don't seem unhappy.

Pause.

HARRY   Is there any particular reason that you're removing your clothes?

MOO *continues.*

HARRY   Is this supposed to be significant?

MOO *advances toward him.*

HARRY   Well, you could at least say something.

MOO   *(seductively)* Hello, Harry.

HARRY   Hello, Moo.

MOO   *(puts her hand on HARRY'S groin)* And how are you, today?

HARRY   *(removes her hand)* Fine, thank you.

MOO   That's good. You seem fine. You seem very well, in fact.

HARRY   I'm worried about you, Moo.

MOO   Don't worry, Harry. You worry too
                much. *(kisses him)*

                HARRY responds reluctantly.

MOO   Now, tell me you're my brother.

HARRY   I'm your brother.

                MOO *kisses him again.*

Act One, Scene Twenty

HARRY *and* MAUDE GORMLEY.

MAUDE	Do you think I should get a nose job?

No response from HARRY.

MAUDE	Well — do you?
HARRY	*(looks up)* No. I don't.
MAUDE	Why not?
HARRY	Your nose is fine the way it is.
MAUDE	I don't know, Harry. It's all bent over to one side. See.
HARRY	Looks okay to me.
MAUDE	Nah. It's all twisted. I think I should get a nose job.
HARRY	Okay. Get a nose job.
MAUDE	But will you love me?
HARRY	Pardon?
MAUDE	I'll look different then. Will you still love me with a nose job?
HARRY	I hadn't thought about it.

MAUDE   Do you really think my nose looks funny?

HARRY   No. I think it looks fine.

MAUDE   Really?

HARRY   Yes.

MAUDE   Not too bent?

HARRY   No.

> *Pause.*

MAUDE   I wonder how much a nose job would cost.

> HARRY *looks up.*

MAUDE   What if it's expensive? Could you afford it?

HARRY   Probably.

MAUDE   Maybe, I will get one done. I really don't like my nose, Harry.

HARRY   Mmmmmmmmhmmmmm.

MAUDE   I think it's ugly. It's a blot upon my face. You know. A real blot.

HARRY   Mmmmmmmmmm.

> *Pause.*

MAUDE   Have you always thought my nose was ugly?

> HARRY *gets up, walks over to* MAUDE, *picks her up and throws her down the stairs.*

Act One, Scene Twenty-one

Hospital room. MOO, DOCTOR *and* NURSE.

DOCTOR I'm terribly sorry, Mrs. Parker. I don't know how to say this. I'm afraid I must apologize.

MOO What?

DOCTOR I said I'm sorry. Really very terribly sorry.

MOO Sorry.

DOCTOR Yes. Sorry.

MOO Oh. *(pause)* Why?

DOCTOR It's all been a terrible mistake. We're very sorry, aren't we, Nurse?

NURSE Oh yes, we are.

DOCTOR You see and oh, it's some embarrassment to us.

NURSE Yes — it is.

DOCTOR Well, we have discovered that you have sisters. And I must apologize for not believing your story. That you really do have sisters.

MOO   Sisters?

DOCTOR   Yes. I thought that Mr. Parker's
                 prolonged absence was suspicious, and so I
                 decided to look up the names you'd given
                 us in the telephone book and I called Mrs.
                 MacDowell and she said yes, indeed, she
                 was your mother and they'd been looking
                 for you for the last five years. They didn't
                 look too hard, apparently, because you'd
                 run off with Mr. Parker and told them not
                 to come looking for you. Still, it was a
                 long time. Is your family often like that?

MOO   Who?

DOCTOR   So, your sister, Sarah, is coming to pick
                 you up.

MOO   My sister.

DOCTOR   Yes.

MOO   You're sure I have a sister.

DOCTOR   Yes.

MOO   And Harry is not my brother.

DOCTOR   No, of course not.

MOO   Harry is my husband.

DOCTOR   Yes. So, it's all settled. We'll get your
                 things. *(motions for* NURSE *to leave)*

MOO   Where is Harry?

DOCTOR   Oh. Well. Now, that's another problem which I didn't really want to broach quite yet.

MOO   Where is Harry?

DOCTOR   Well, we received this in the mail last week. We didn't show it to you because we thought it might upset you.

MOO   What is it?

DOCTOR   It's a postcard.

MOO   Let's see it.

DOCTOR *hands it to her.*

MOO   It's a desert island.

DOCTOR   Yes, pretty isn't it? Now, let's have it back.

MOO   *(turns it over and reads)*
"On the black sands of Montserrat,
People live and die,
How bout that.

Harry."

DOCTOR   Your sister will come for you, tomorrow.

MOO   Where is Montserrat?

DOCTOR   We'll get your clothes.

MOO   *(stares at postcard)* I'll have to find him.

DOCTOR   Yes. He owes us money.

Act One, Scene Twenty-two

	MOO *and her family;* MR. *and* MRS. MACDOWELL, SARAH *and* DOROTHY.

Poor Moo comes Home

SARAH	Oh Moo, you poor dear.
DITTY	I think it's absolutely dreadful. Don't you agree, Father?
MR. MACDOWELL	Oh yes. Dreadful.
MOO	Do we have an atlas?
MRS. MACDOWELL	Yes, dear, it's on the shelf.
	MOO *goes to shelf, gets atlas and leafs through it while everyone else is talking.*
MRS. MACDOWELL	*(with great pronouncement)* He was a R-E-A-A-L RRRotter.
SARAH	I knew he was a rotter the moment I laid eyes on him.
DITTY	So did I.
SARAH	No, you didn't. You would have done just what Mooley did.
DITTY	Would not.

SARAH	Would too.
MRS. MACDOWELL	I never liked him. He had shifty black eyes.
MOO	They were large and blue, Mother.
MRS. MACDOWELL	Still, they were shifty. I don't care how large they were. They moved around a lot. I didn't trust him as far as I could spit. None of us liked him.
MOO	Father liked him.
SARAH	That doesn't count. Father likes everyone.
MR. MACDOWELL	I think it's dreadful.
DITTY	Poor Moo.
SARAH	Poor Moo.
MRS. MACDOWELL	He was a real rotter.
MR. MACDOWELL	Handsome bastard.
SARAH	Oh, did you think he was handsome. I suppose so if you liked that type.
MRS. MACDOWELL	He must have hypnotized you, Moo. That's all I can say.

He must have hypnotized you

MOO
Mother, why is it when anything untoward happens, it means someone's been hypnotized.

MRS. MACDOWELL
It's the only rational explanation for it. Otherwise, I can't account for why you ran off with that dreadful man.

MOO
Maybe I loved him.

MRS. MACDOWELL
That's just it. You couldn't possibly have loved such a man. He must have hypnotized you.

MOO
I don't want to discuss it.

MRS. MACDOWELL
We're not discussing it. We're sympathizing. Stop flipping through that atlas.

DITTY
Poor Moo.

MOO
Will you stop saying that!

MRS. MACDOWELL
Well, it's all right now, Mooley. You're back home where you belong. We won't say another word about it.

Long pause.

MRS. MACDOWELL
It's unbelievable. Inconceivable that anyone could do such a thing. Why would he sign you away like that?

MOO	Maybe, he thought I had money.
MRS. MACDOWELL	Yes. But we have money. You don't have money. He must have realized that.
MOO	I don't know why, then.
MR. MACDOWELL	I think it's dreadful.
DITTY	Poor Moo.
SARAH	What a rotter.
MOO	Where is Montserrat?
MRS. MACDOWELL	Pardon?
MR. MACDOWELL	Pardon?
MOO	Where is Montserrat?
MRS. MACDOWELL	Oh, I don't know.
MOO	Do you know where it is, Father?
MR. MACDOWELL	What?
MOO	Forget it.
MRS. MACDOWELL	Africa, I think.

MOO	Are you sure?
MRS. MACDOWELL	I think it's off Africa. Or is it South America? Oh well, it's down there somewhere. Why?
MOO	I think I'd like to get away for a while.
MRS. MACDOWELL	You've just been away.
MOO	I was locked up. It's not quite the same thing.
MRS. MACDOWELL	I suppose you could use a vacation. *(to* MR. MACDOWELL) What do you think, dear?
MR. MACDOWELL	Mmmm?
MRS. MACDOWELL	Moo wants to go away. What do you think?
MR. MACDOWELL	She's just been away.
MRS. MACDOWELL	Yes, yes, dear, we've been through all that. She wants to go — where do you want to go, dear?
MOO	I'm not sure.

MRS.
MACDOWELL   I think you better take Ditty. I don't want
              you travelling by yourself. You're not
              well.

DITTY   If she's going to Montserrat, I'm not
              going.

MRS.
MACDOWELL   Why not, dear?

DITTY   In the first place, we don't know where it
              is. In the second —

MOO   DAMMIT!!! IT'S NOT IN HERE! IT'S
              NOT IN HERE!!! *(slams book)*

Act One, Scene Twenty-three

HARRY, *in tropical paradise.*

HARRY   Some people eat you alive. They'll
consume you utterly if you let them.
They'll pick you up, take you in, give you
a good mulching over and then, spit you
out, till there's nothing left but little bones.
And then they wonder why they don't
want you anymore. And the worst of it is
you don't know this is going to happen
when you meet them. A sign should be
there. Bells should ring. An angel of
mercy should shoot down from the sky and
wave flags and banners. But no, nothing
happens. You blithely saunter into your
doom because at that particular moment,
you have nothing better to do.

Moo. Sweet, demure when I first met her.
Well, as demure as you can get when
you're brandishing a .22 calibre rifle. That
should have tipped me off. But no, I was
feeling rather cocky that day. Sure of
myself. So, there it was, that sweet, small
little woman gets hold of a small part of
my soul and, before I know it, she's in
there with an oyster knife, trying to pry the
whole thing out. I'm sorry. Sometimes, it
all comes down to a question of pure,
simple survival. Dammit. I wish I didn't
love her. I'd give my soul not to love her.
I'm fed to the teeth with loving her.

Act One, Scene Twenty-four

> *Montserrat. Hotel room.* HARRY, *in bed. There is a knock at the door.*

HARRY   Who's there?

VOICE   Room service.

HARRY   *(goes to answer door)* I didn't ask for room service.

MOO   *(stands in doorway)* Hello, Harry.

HARRY   Jesus.

MOO   Aren't you going to invite me in?

HARRY   Oh — well — ah — *(grabs her, drags her in, frisks her)*

MOO   What are you doing?

HARRY   Sorry — it's just that —

MOO   Did you think I had a gun or something?

HARRY   It crossed my mind.

MOO   I'm not angry with you, Harry.

HARRY   You should be, Moo.

MOO   I forgive you, Harry.

HARRY   I don't want to be forgiven.

MOO   It's all right, Harry. I forgive you. We
        can start all over again.

HARRY   I don't want to start over again. I want
        you to forget about me. Hate me.
        Anything. Just stay away from me.

MOO   I don't hate you, Harry.

HARRY   I had you committed, Moo. I put you in a
        loony bin. You might still be there.

MOO   I got out.

HARRY   I should have figured that.

MOO   And I've come back to you.

HARRY   Christ. Where's your pride? Don't you
        have any dignity. Can't you muster up
        some self-respect —

MOO   Harry, you know you love me.

HARRY   I don't, Moo.

MOO   You're just saying that.

HARRY   I married you for your money.

MOO   And you're welcome to it.

HARRY   I don't want it, anymore. I don't want
        you!

MOO	You just don't want to admit it. It frightens you, doesn't it? I have a power over you and —
HARRY	You don't have any power over me, Moo.
MOO	It frightens you.
HARRY	I was unfaithful to you, Moo. Those nights when I came home at 4:30, I was screwing Maude Gormley.
MOO	It was just your way, Harry.
HARRY	What!
MOO	You had to prove to yourself that you didn't love me.
HARRY	I succeeded.
MOO	So, you had trivial affairs.
HARRY	They weren't trivial, Moo. Maude was a great screw.
MOO	A screw, though. That's all she was.
HARRY	I wouldn't say that, exactly.
MOO	Why do I frighten you, Harry? *(starts to unbutton blouse)*
HARRY	You don't frighten me. Ah, what are you doing?
MOO	I'm unbuttoning my blouse.
HARRY	Stop it.

MOO	Why, Harry? You're not attracted to me. You just said so.
HARRY	Yes —
MOO	So, it shouldn't make any difference to you if I unbutton my blouse. It's not going to affect you. Not Harry. *(removes shoe, puts leg up on chair close to* HARRY, *removes stocking slowly)*
HARRY	I would like you to stop.
MOO	It's very hot in here, Harry. You shouldn't have come to Montserrat in the off-season. *(removes other stocking)*
HARRY	Jesus.
MOO	What's the matter, Harry? Am I affecting you? *(performs slow strip tease)*
HARRY	No. You're not!
MOO	Good. I'm glad. That's a load off my mind.

        MOO *is stripped to bra and pants.*
        She approaches HARRY.

HARRY	Get away from me.
MOO	Why are you afraid of me?
HARRY	Dammit. I am not afraid of you.
MOO	Prove it.

HARRY   DAMN YOU, WHAT DOES IT TAKE
                   TO CONVINCE YOU!! *(grabs* MOO *by
                   the shoulders and shakes her)*

                        MOO *interrupts him by putting her
                        arms around him and kissing him.
                        HARRY resists at first, then, responds.
                        They embrace passionately.*

MOO   You love me, Harry. You know that.

HARRY   *(wearily)* Yes, Moo. I love you.

MOO   Good.

Act One, Scene Twenty-five

*Early morning. HARRY and MOO
are in bed. He wakes up and glances
at her. She is sleeping soundly. He
sneaks out of bed, starts to pack
clothes. She moans. He freezes, waits
for a movement from her. She goes
back to sleep. He hurries, finishes
packing and steals out the door.*

MOO Mmmmm *(reaches)* Mmmmmm Harry?
Harry? *(sits up)*
HAAAAAAAAAAAAAARRRRRY!!!!!!!!

End of Act One

Act Two, Scene One

*1960. HARRY and his third wife,
PATSY, sitting in front of the
television set. He is about 60 years
old. She is slightly younger.*

HARRY — You know, I was a heartbreaker in my youth.

PATSY — You?

HARRY — Don't act so surprised. Yes, I was a cad.

PATSY — Gowan.

HARRY — I was. A real heartbreaker.

PATSY — AAAW come off it, Harry, you're a real sweet guy.

HARRY — Now, maybe. But not then. I've been married twice, you know.

PATSY — I'm sure you didn't mean it, dear.

HARRY — Yes. I did. Both times. For a year there, I was a bigamist. Saw both of them. Did a lot of commuting.

PATSY — You're a kidder, Harry.

HARRY — I threw my second wife down the stairs.

PATSY — Did she upset you?

HARRY   Well, yeah. I guess so. I guess that's why I threw her down the stairs. Can't really remember why. Curious, isn't it? I could always call her up and ask her. She'd remember.

PATSY   You must have had a reason, Harry.

HARRY   I think I was mad at her.

PATSY   There you are.

HARRY   You're a wonderful woman, Patsy.

PATSY   Harry.

         Pause.

HARRY   I.put my first wife in an insane asylum.

PATSY   Why was that, dear?

HARRY   She was crazy. I was mad at her. Something to do at the time.

PATSY   I'm sure you weren't thinking, dear.

HARRY   I knew what I was doing.

PATSY   Harry.

HARRY   You don't believe me, do you? I threw her in, locked the door and threw away the key.

PATSY   Did she get out?

HARRY   Oh yeah.

PATSY	Well, no harm done then, is there?
HARRY	No. No harm done. *(pause)* She's mad as a hatter, now, though.
PATSY	Have you seen her recently?
HARRY	No.
PATSY	How do you know, then?
HARRY	She was crazy when I last saw her.
PATSY	When was that?
HARRY	Oh. Let's see, now. Twenty years ago.
PATSY	You don't know then, do you? She might not be mad. She might be dead for all you know.
HARRY	That's true. She might be dead.
PATSY	And if she's dead, then it's all over and done with and you've nothing to worry about.
HARRY	That's true, Patsy. That's very true.

Pause.

HARRY	What if she's alive?
PATSY	You should send her a Christmas card and let her know you're thinking of her.
HARRY	I don't think so.

PATSY   Huh.

HARRY   I don't think I want to send her a
               Christmas card.

PATSY   Suit yourself. Everyone likes to get cards,
               though.

                    Pause.

HARRY   Did anyone ever put a bullet through your
               brain, Patsy?

PATSY   You're a kidder, Harry.

Act Two, Scene Two

HARRY, *alone on stage.*

HARRY   I dream about her. Not all the time, of course. But, she's a constant in my life. Years pass and I'm not even aware of it. She's still right where I left her. Raging at me. Loving me. Cursing me for my lack of faith. Faith — coming from her, that's a good one. Most suspicious woman I ever met. Why did I not have faith, she said. I couldn't. I knew she would suck the very life out of me. It's safer this way. Safer to seek shelter. In someone else's flaccid heart.

Act Two, Scene Three

> MOO'S *sixtieth birthday party. There is one main table with* MOO, WALLY, DITTY, SARAH *and* CHARLIE, SARAH'S *husband,* JANE, SARAH'S *daughter and* SUSAN, JANE'S *daughter. The other relatives are at other tables in the room.*

CROWD   SPEECH SPEECH! COME ON, CHARLIE!!

CHARLIE   *(rises)* Hhhhhhhmph Hmmm. Today, erhem, erhem we are celebrating the, erhem, sixtieth birthday...

MOO   You don't have to say which birthday, Charlie.

CHARLIE   Right. Hemm, hemm. Right. The birthday of a most venerable woman...

MOO   I'm not a Chinese ancestor, Charlie.

CHARLIE   Right.

SARAH   Let him get on with it, Mooley.

CHARLIE   Woman, erhem, er, er, a woman — uh — *(pause)* who stands on her own, of course, not simply an —

> WALLY *is pawing* MOO.

MOO   Hooooooh! Wally! *(giggles)*

CHARLIE	Yes, yes, of course, a woman of many diverse talents.
MOO	Stop it, Wally! *(giggles)*
WALLY	*(snorting laugh)* Ooooooooh Mooley...
CHARLIE	Painter. Many of you young people might not realize that your Great Aunt Moo was a student of Emily Carr.
SUSAN	Who's Emily Carr?
JANE	Ssssh. Susan.
CHARLIE	Pardon? Did someone say something?
JANE	You shouldn't interrupt your grandfather when he's making a speech.
SUSAN	But Mummy, who's Emily Carr?
JANE	She painted trees. Now shut up.
CHARLIE	Now where was I?
SUSAN	Emily Carr. She painted trees.
CHARLIE	Oh yes. *(with great gravity)* Emily Carr painted trees. *(pause)* I don't think I intended to say that.
MOO	EEEEEEEK! Wally! My God, you're disgusting.
WALLY	Have another shot, Mooley. *(pours her more wine)*

CHARLIE   And Moo painted trees, too. Yes and
           some people say hers were better than
           Emily's. Hem, hem.

DITTY   You've got that story all wrong, Charlie.

CHARLIE   Mmmmph.

DITTY   I painted trees. Moo couldn't paint to save
           her life.

MOO   Ditty, you dodo brain. I painted that tree
           and you know it.

DITTY   You did not.

MOO   Did too!

DITTY   Did not!

MOO   Did too!

SARAH   Would you two please shut up! It's your
           birthday, Mooley. Remember that and
           behave yourself.

CHARLIE   Yes — well — where was I? Aside from
           being a painter, Moo is a remarkable cook.

DITTY   Remarkable is right.

MOO   *(to* DITTY) What did you say?

CHARLIE   We have been treated to the world's
           cuisines...

DITTY   Dogfish.

CHARLIE   At the capable hands of Moo.

DITTY   No one else would try and make a meal
                 out of dogfish.

SARAH   Ditty!

CHARLIE   And today, hem, hem —

                 WALLY *tries to pull* MOO'S *dress off
                 her shoulder.*

SUSAN   Mummy, what is that old man trying to
                 do?

JANE   He's making a speech. Sssssh.

SUSAN   Not Grandpa. Him! *(points to* WALLY)

JANE   He's trying to pull her dress off. Now
                 shut up!

SUSAN   But why, Mummy?

MOO   I'm an old fucking woman as of today.

                 WALLY *continues to maul* MOO.

CHARLIE   She's an old fucking...

SARAH   Charlie!

CHARLIE   Oh sorry. Right — hem, hem —

SARAH   A toast, dear.

CHARLIE   Right. So, let's propose a toast to Moo.
                 Sixty years old today. Will you all please
                 rise.

> EVERYONE, *except for* MOO *and*
> WALLY, *rise.*

CHARLIE   *(with glass raised)* To Moo!

CROWD   To Moo!

> CHARLIE *turns round to face* MOO,
> *who is under the table with* WALLY.

MOO   *(giggling)* Oh Wally!

> WALLY *snorts.*

SUSAN   What a creepy old man.

MOO   I'm an old fucking woman as of today.

WALLY   You'll never be too old for me, Mooley.

MOO   A corpse wouldn't be too old for you,
SnortSnort.

CHARLIE   Yes. Well. To Moo.

CROWD   To Moo.

MOO   I'll drink to that. *(giggles)*

> *They politely try to ignore the*
> *commotion under the table.* JANE
> *walks over to* SARAH *and drags her*
> *off to one side.*

JANE   This is disgraceful. I asked you not to
invite him.

SARAH	Moo likes him.
JANE	That is apparent.
SARAH	It's her birthday.
JANE	Must she celebrate here and now.
SARAH	I don't think she's doing anything wrong.

MOO *giggles.*

JANE	Have you looked, Mother?
SARAH	No. Have you?
JANE	Certainly not!
DITTY	I'll look.
SARAH	Ditty!
SUSAN	*(walks up to* JANE) Why is she called Moo, Mummy?
JANE	Not now, dear.
SUSAN	Why have I never seen her before?
DITTY	You're not seeing much of her now, either.

SUSAN *wanders over to main table.*

JANE	SUSAN!

SUSAN *wanders back.*

JANE	She does a lot of travelling.

SUSAN	Gee, that must be exciting. I'd like to travel.
MOO	*(rises from beneath table)* That's enough, Wally. *(giggles)* Jane, little Janie, did you arrive late? I didn't see you. Wally's been very distracting. How the hell are ya?
JANE	Mmmmph.
MOO	Oh Jane — sorry — oh sorry, Jane, gotta watch the language in front of the kid.
JANE	My daughter, Susan.
MOO	So, you two finally had a kid. *(to* SUSAN) Hi, kiddo, I'm your aunt Moo-Cow.
SUSAN	You have a funny name.
MOO	Don't we all, kiddo. Don't we all. Sarah, this is a great party. Just great. Almost makes me forget I'm an old trout, now. Never too old to play with Wally. Isn't he disgusting? I think he's the most repulsive man I've ever come across. And that's saying something.
JANE	He certainly is vile.
MOO	Hey Wally, SnortSnort, what are you doing with that piano?
WALLY	Tuning.
MOO	Let's see. *(goes over to join* WALLY)

JANE   She gets more garrulous every year.

SUSAN   What's garrulous, Mummy?

SARAH   She's had a very unhappy life.

JANE   That's no excuse.

> *There is a knock at the door.* SUSAN *goes to answer it.*

SUSAN   *(returns)* Mummy, there's a telegram for Aunt Moo.

JANE   You give it to her, dear.

SUSAN   *(walks over to* MOO *and* WALLY*)* Oh Auntie Moo — here's a telegram for you.

MOO   *(takes it)* Thanks kiddo. *(opens it, reads and screams)* AAAAAAAAaaaaahhh! (rails around the room, knocks tables over, hurls furniture about) THE BASTARD THE FUCKING BASTARD!!! *(runs out of the room)*

SARAH   Moo?

WALLY   Moo?

SARAH   What's got into her?

DITTY   She's had too much to drink.

JANE   The telegram.

WALLY   *(walks over to telegram, opens it and reads)*
"On the white sands of Micronesia,
People live and die,
Just to please ya."

(looks up, confused) Who's Harry?

Act Two, Scene Four

> MOO, *aged 65 and* SUSAN, *aged 13.*
> MOO *is wearing a muumuu and beads*
> *about her neck. She is sitting cross-*
> *legged on the floor and drinking gin.*

MOO   Never give the suckers a break, kiddo.
Know what I mean?

SUSAN   I wish you were my mother, Aunt Moo.

MOO   Pardon?

SUSAN   I do. I hate my mother. She never lets me
do anything I want. And she's so straight.

MOO   Straight. *(pours more gin)*

SUSAN   You know, everything follows in a straight
line for her. Cause and effect. Cause and
effect. It's so boring. I hate it.

MOO   Your mother's a special case, kiddo.
Sarah spent a lot of time raising her to be
nice and proper. Ruined her for good.

SUSAN   Why couldn't you be my mother. You'd
be a perfect mother for me.

MOO   No, I wouldn't.

SUSAN   Why, Aunt Moo?

MOO   We've got more important things to
discuss, kiddo. Now, what was I saying?

SUSAN   Never give the suckers a break.

MOO   Right. And the only thing men understand is sex. Know what I mean?

SUSAN   I think so.

MOO   And you don't give it to them. Here's a little song you should know. *(sings)*

"I'm just gonna keep sitting on it,
fore I'm gonna give it away."

Whenever you get thoughtful, just sing that song. It'll smarten you up.

SUSAN   I'm only thirteen, Aunt Moo.

MOO   They start them young in Micronesia. Now, I've been taking these anthropology courses.

SUSAN   Anthropology?

MOO   Study of man. It's essential these days. Particularly, if you're a woman. Now, some of these books claim that man is essentially a wanderer. The men are out there hunting and stuff while the woman sits at home and watches the camp. But other books say that there are societies where it's totally reversed. The women are the ones who are out screwing around while the men have to do all the boring stuff.

SUSAN   Micronesia?

MOO   Samoa. So, the key thing to remember is don't get married and don't let any man run your life. Right?

SUSAN   Right.

MOO   I'll drink to that. *(sips gin)*

SUSAN   So, what should we do?

MOO   Do?

SUSAN   Yeah. What should we do? How should we start?

MOO   Hell, I don't know. Do we have to start right away? Can't we sit and talk about it for a while.

SUSAN   I think we should start.

MOO   Well, you go right ahead, kiddo. You go right ahead.

Act Two, Scene Five

SUSAN *and her mother,* JANE.

SUSAN	I want to be just like Aunt Moo when I grow up.
JANE	No, you don't.
SUSAN	Yes, I do, Mum. Boy, remember the way she threw that furniture around. That was fun!
JANE	That wasn't funny, Susan. Your Aunt Moo is a very sick woman.
SUSAN	I want to be just like her. I'll never get married. I'll have boyfriends, instead. Well, not like Wally. He was really repulsive. I'll get some nice boyfriends and I can do whatever I like with them.
JANE	Don't you want to get married, dear?
SUSAN	Like you, Mum?
JANE	Well — yes.
SUSAN	No way. What a bore. What a fucking bore.
JANE	WHAT DID YOU SAY!
SUSAN	Sorry.

JANE   I don't like the way you visit her all the time. It's affecting you. What do you talk about, anyway?

SUSAN   Everything. Women's rights, labour unions, female oppression —

JANE   She looks absolutely ridiculous. In that stupid muumuu and wearing those silly beads around her neck. Who does she think she is, anyway?

SUSAN   She's liberated, Ma.

JANE   The hell she is. She's obsessed.

Act Two, Scene Six

> DITTY *is at* MOO's *apartment.*
> *They are hanging curtains while*
> *standing precariously on a bookcase.*

DITTY   We worry about you, Mooley.

MOO   Who worries about me?

DITTY   Sarah and I.

MOO   I'm happy by myself.

DITTY   You live like a hermit, dear. What if
             something happened to you? Who'd ever
             find out about it?

MOO   No one, I suppose.

DITTY   And what would happen to you?

MOO   I'd die, I guess.

DITTY   That's not good enough, Moo.

MOO   Can you pass me some of those curtain
             hooks?

DITTY   *(reaches down to a ledge on the bookcase,*
             picks up some hooks) You drink too
             much.

MOO   It's none of your business, Dit.

DITTY   We're your family.

MOO   I don't want you. Doesn't that ever dawn
                   on you. What good are you, anyway.
                   You're always trying to have me put away
                   somewhere.

DITTY   Harry did that, Moo.

MOO   Well, what about this old folks home you
                   want to stick me into.

DITTY   It's not an old folks home. It's a hotel for
                   retired people.

MOO   Why me? Why not you? You're older
                   than me.

DITTY   But, you don't have anyone, Moo. It's
                   bad for someone to be by themselves as
                   much as you are.

MOO   You know, I've never stopped looking for
                   him, Dit. I've travelled all over the world
                   looking for him.

DITTY   That was silly of you, Moo.

MOO   Obsessive. I can't help it.

DITTY   He's living in Seattle.

MOO   WHAT!

DITTY   He married Maude Gormley and he's living
                   in Seattle.

MOO   MAUDE!

DITTY   I thought you knew that, Moo.

MOO	Maude Gormley.
DITTY	Everyone knew, Moo. Didn't anyone tell you?
MOO	AAAAAAGH! *(falls off the bookcase)*
DITTY	OH MOO! OH MOOLEY!! *(teeters on top of bookcase)* Oh dear, Moocow. *(jumps, lands on* MOO*)*
MOO	OOOOOOOOWWW!
DITTY	Of course, I think they got divorced and I think he's married someone else. He threw her down the stairs. Maude, that is. Not his new wife.

MOO *groans.*

DITTY	Oh Moo, I'm sorry to upset you. I thought you knew. We all thought you knew.
MOO	Get off.
DITTY	She was very angry. Enough was enough, she said. My God, that was years ago. It all seems like yesterday.
MOO	GET OFF.
DITTY	Pardon, Moo.
MOO	My hip.
DITTY	Oh Moo. We do worry about you. *(gets off)* Are you all right?

MOO	Hospital.
DITTY	Pardon, Moo?
MOO	Hospital. I can't move.
DITTY	Oh dear. Oh no. Oh now, Mooley. Oh dear. Oh no.
MOO	Call the hospital.
DITTY	Oh dear. I always panic. Oh dear, where's the phone?
MOO	JESUS F. CHRIST.
DITTY	Don't get upset, Moo. Lie still. Keep calm. Remember, I'm here with you.
MOO	JESUS F. CHRIST. SINGAPORE, HONG KONG, MONTSERRAT, MICRONESIA. ALL THIS TIME IT'S BEEN GODDAMN SEATTLE. JESUS F. CHRIST.

Act Two, Scene Seven

Nursing home. MOO *is in bed.*

Surprise for Miss Parker

NURSE	We have a surprise for you, Miss Parker.
MOO	Mrs. Parker. Goddammit!
NURSE	My, my, let's not be cranky.
MOO	I can be as cranky as I like. I'm paying you to let me be cranky.
NURSE	Now, Miss Parker, your relatives are paying for your stay here.
MOO	Big deal. Goddamned hell hole. Why am I with all these old people, anyway? Why aren't I with the broken hip people? I hate hospitals.

This isn't a hospital

NURSE	This isn't a hospital.
MOO	What!
NURSE	This is a nursing home.
MOO	WHAT! *(starts to get up)*
NURSE	Now please, Miss Parker. Don't move or you'll aggravate that hip.
MOO	Get out of my way. *(tries to get up)* OW! *(falls back in bed)*

NURSE	Now, see what I said. *(to doorway)* Oh, she's really in a bad state. I don't think she should see you.
DITTY	Nonsense! Moo! Moo, it's me.
MOO	Get away from me, you old cow!
DITTY	Oh Mooley, what have they done to you?
MOO	They? You! You mean.
DITTY	Oh Moo, so angry.
MOO	Get your long false teeth away from me.
DITTY	Oh Mooley, what's happened to you? And your hip? Is your hip all right?
MOO	Who put you up to it? Did Sarah put you up to it?
DITTY	I don't know what you're talking about. *(to* NURSE*)* Is she all right?
NURSE	About the same.
MOO	*(mimics)* Is your hip all right? You jumped on it. You should know.
DITTY	No Mooley, I didn't jump on your hip. I fell.
MOO	Fell! Ha!
SARAH	*(enters)* Sorry, I'm late. Moo darling, how are you?

Handwritten annotations: "Oh Moo so angry" (above DITTY line); "I had to get down somehow." (below MOO's "Fell! Ha!")

MOO   It was your idea, wasn't it? Lock me up for good this time.

SARAH   *(to* DITTY) What's she talking about?

MOO   *(to* DITTY) Don't try to deny it. I saw you looking at me. Goddammit, you paused, counted to three and then you jumped.

DITTY   I did not jump on your hip.

MOO   I watched you from the ground. I saw your lips move.

DITTY   Well, whose fault was it that I was on top of your rickety old bookcase.

MOO   I asked you to help me hang the curtains. I didn't ask you to jump on my hip.

DITTY   Well, what was I to do. I had to get down somehow.

MOO   You could have jumped on your own hip. You didn't need to jump on mine.

Are you going senile?

SARAH   Moo? Are you going senile?

MOO   So help me, you may think you've got me right where you want me. But I'm getting out of here if it's the last thing I do.

SARAH   Yes, dear. Whatever you say, dear.

MOO   Don't humour me. I mean it.

DITTY   She's going senile, isn't she, Sarah?

SARAH	Yes, dear. I'm afraid she is.
MOO	SENILE!!
SARAH	Too much gin.
MOO	THAT'S IT. OUT, OUT! EVERYBODY OUT!!!

Act Two, Scene Eight

HARRY *sits in a large black easy chair. There is a large globe on a stand beside the chair. He spins it occasionally.*

HARRY   Sometimes, I send her postcards. Spite, I suppose. It's a thing with me. Express the universe on a four by six card. Of course, I make them totally banal. I know that will irritate her. I like to go to small far-off places of the globe *(laughs)* and send her postcards. *(laughs)* And I never write: "Having a wonderful time. Wish you were here." *(laughs)* I never say: 'Wish you were here." *(laughs)*

Act Two, Scene Nine

> MOO *and her son,* DOUGALL. *He is wearing a hat and playing with a capgun.*

DOUGALL   Mummy, when's Daddy coming home?

MOO   I've told you, kiddo. He's not coming home.

DOUGALL   Are you going to Bora Bora again? Can I stay with Aunt Sarah and Jane while you're away?

MOO   I'm not going to Bora Bora.

DOUGALL   Why not, Mummy?

MOO   You only go to those places once, kiddo.

DOUGALL   When are you going to go away?

MOO   I'm not going away.

DOUGALL   Why not, Mummy?

MOO   I'm tired of it. I've had enough.

DOUGALL   Oh. *(pause)* I could try and find him. When I grow up, I'll find Daddy for you.

MOO   I don't want him.

DOUGALL   Why not? What's wrong with him?

MOO   He's not here, is he. That's enough for a
               start.

DOUGALL   Jane says Daddy ran away. Did Daddy
               run away?

MOO   Look kiddo, I don't want to talk about it.
               It's all over and done with.

                    Pause.

DOUGALL   You got another postcard, Mummy.

MOO   What!

DOUGALL   It came in the mail today. I put it on the
               mantlepiece. Where's Banyu Wangi?

                    MOO *gets up.*

DOUGALL   Mummy, mummy. Where're you going,
               Mummy?

MOO   *(rushes out)* See you later, kiddo.

Act Two, Scene Ten

Hotel shack in Banyu Wangi. MOO arrives, soaking wet, with suitcase. The DESK CLERK is asleep. She rings the bell.

CLERK   *(starts up)* Oh! Oh! Many pardons. We no get visitors in Banyu Wangi in rainy season and now, two in one month.

MOO   Yes. Where is he?

CLERK   He?

MOO   Other visitor. Him, man, no?

CLERK   Yes.

MOO   Where is he? What room?

CLERK   Him gone. Him no like rain.

MOO   When did he leave?

CLERK   Gone. Long ago.

MOO   When?

CLERK   You want room?

MOO   I'm not sure yet. When did he go?

CLERK   Rooms cost twelve renigos.

MOO   When did the man go?

CLERK	What man?
MOO	Man. Named Harry Parker. His name Harry Parker. No?

> CLERK *stares at* MOO.

MOO	Oh. I see. *(takes out money)*
CLERK	*(takes money)* Tuan Parker left three weeks ago.
MOO	Where'd he go?

> CLERK *pauses.* MOO *pulls out more money.*

CLERK	Me not know. Me think other islands.
MOO	That's all there is here. Nothing but bloody islands!
CLERK	Him go further east. Easter Island. Ha ha. Small joke.

> MOO *takes back a bill.*

CLERK	Sorry. Me think he go to Atapupu. Him might have gone to Pugobengo but me think he go to Atapupu. Him mention Kotomobagu. Him go to visit Tejakula then to Klungklung then he stay in Pugobengo. That when he mention Kotomabagu.

> MOO *moans, collapses in nearby chair.*

CLERK But me try Atapupu. Atapupu nice. No
rainy season now. Oh! Tuana lady no
feel good. Here, you go to bed. Nice
rooms here. You rest. *(draws her up)*
Room three good. No roaches. You like.
No jiggers. Some earwig, though. Stop
up ears before sleeping. Otherwise earwig
make home and nasty nasty. You get good
rest.

CLERK *leads* MOO *out.*

Act Two, Scene Eleven

> MOO *is unpacking.* DOUGALL
> *watches her.*

MOO *(brings out a small stuffed alligator)* There you are, kiddo. A nice stuffed alligator.

DOUGALL Where's Daddy?

MOO Your guess is as good as mine, kiddo.

DOUGALL I want Daddy.

MOO You can't have Daddy. How bout a nice stuffed alligator, instead?

DOUGALL I don't want a stuffed alligator. I want to see Daddy. You get to see Daddy. Why can't I see Daddy?

MOO Who told you I saw your father?

DOUGALL Jane.

MOO She's telling you stories.

DOUGALL I wish I had a father.

MOO Oh Dougall. Stop it.

DOUGALL But I'd like a father.

MOO I brought you a shrunken head.

DOUGALL You did! Oh Mummy!! Where is it, Mummy! Where is it!!!

MOO *pulls out a shrunken head.*

DOUGALL   Oh. *(draws away)*

MOO   What's the matter, kiddo?

DOUGALL   *(whispers)* Is that Daddy?

MOO   Of course not.

DOUGALL   Who is it, then?

MOO   I don't know. It's not anyone. It's a shrunken head.

     DOUGALL *stares at the head.* MOO *continues unpacking.*

DOUGALL   Daddy, is that you? Was Mummy mean to you in Borneo?

MOO   *(hearing DOUGALL say "Daddy", stops unpacking and watches him)* WHAT THE HELL DO YOU THINK YOU'RE DOING!

DOUGALL   Oh! I'm just playing with him, Mummy.

MOO   You just called that shrunken head, "Daddy." That is not your Daddy, Dougall. Do you hear me?

DOUGALL   Yes, Mummy.

MOO   It's a horrible thing, anyway. I should never have brought it back. *(takes it from DOUGALL)*

DOUGALL   No, Mummy, no! Please let me have it.
             Please, please, please!

MOO   No. This one's going in a drawer. You're
             too young. It'll just give you bad dreams.
             (puts it in a drawer)

DOUGALL   Please, Mummy, please!

MOO   NO! *(closes drawer)* And that's final.
             Maybe, when you're older. Now stop
             blubbering and play with your alligator.

DOUGALL   Yes, Mummy.

             MOO *starts to leave.*

DOUGALL   Where're you going, Mummy?

MOO   Mummy's going downstairs to pour herself
             a good stiff drink.

DOUGALL   Oh.

             DOUGALL *waits till* MOO *is gone.*
             He goes over to the drawer, opens it
             and stares at the shrunken head.

Act Two, Scene Twelve

> SARAH, DITTY *and* MOO, *who is gardening.*

SARAH	You know, you really ought to think about getting married again, Moo. All this brooding isn't good for you.
MOO	I'm quite content, Sarah. I have Dougall.

SARAH	That's another thing, Moo. Ditty and I have been noticing and well, we really don't know quite how to put this, but you aren't exactly pleasant to your son.
MOO	What do you mean "pleasant?"
SARAH	Well. Nice, then.
DITTY	You aren't very nice to Dougall.
MOO	Dougall's never told me.
SARAH	No. I don't think he would. Children are like that.
DITTY	I don't even think he knows you're being mean to him.
MOO	Maybe, ladies, the possibility exists and please don't think I'm pressing a point but perhaps I'm not being mean to my son at all. Which is why he hasn't noticed. Which is why I haven't noticed. Which is just something you two meddling farts would imagine.

SARAH	Did you or did you not tell Dougall he was ugly?
MOO	*(to* SARAH) You told Dougall he didn't look like his father. *(to* DITTY) And you told Dougall his father was handsome. So Dougall put two and two together and came to the conclusion that he must be ugly. Which is not far off. He certainly is not an attractive boy.
SARAH	There! Now how can you say that about your own son.
MOO	Because it's true. The boy's homely. Maybe he'll outgrow it. Chances are he won't. But there's always hope.
SARAH	Jane says you told Dougall he was stupid.
MOO	Jane! What does your daughter have to do with it. Anyway, he's not that bright.
SARAH	You can't tell him that.
MOO	Well — do you think Dougall is highly intelligent?
SARAH	He's a dear, sweet boy.
MOO	Yes. But is he highly intelligent?
SARAH	Well — no — he isn't. But I just think that being his mother, you, of all people, should at least think he's intelligent.
MOO	Lie to him, then.

boring

SARAH	Try to be a bit nicer. That's all. Now, Charlie's brother Arthur —
MOO	NO.
SARAH	But Moo, I haven't —
MOO	No. I don't want to meet him. He'll be just like his brother. Boring!
SARAH	Charles and I have been very happy together and I've never found him boring.
MOO	Do you know why that is?
SARAH	Compatibility, I expect.
MOO	No, Osmosis. Now, you're both boring.
SARAH	WELL, I'VE...

Try to be nice.

DITTY	Montserrat.
MOO	What?
DITTY	He's just come back from Montserrat.
SARAH	We thought you'd have a lot to talk about. Just meet him. It can't hurt.
MOO	All right.
SARAH	Good. And Moo?
MOO	Yes, Sarah.
SARAH	Try to be nice.
MOO	Yes, Sarah.

Act Two, Scene Thirteen

MOO *and* DOUGALL.

DOUGALL   Why'd you have to get rid of Daddy?

MOO   That man was not your Daddy, Dougall.

DOUGALL   Well, why'd you get rid of him? I liked Uncle Arthur.

MOO   You hardly knew him.

DOUGALL   He played ball with me.

MOO   I could play ball with you.

DOUGALL   You're never here.

MOO   You could play ball with Jane, then.

DOUGALL   Jane can't catch. And she can't throw, either. What's wrong with Uncle Arthur? He and Uncle Charlie are really funny. They tell good jokes. This guy met this girl and his friend said: 'What's she like?'' and the guy said "Well, she's sort of pretty and she's sort of ugly, so I guess I'd say she was both. PRETTY UGLY!" Ha! Ha! Isn't that funny, Mummy.

MOO   A laugh riot.

DOUGALL   *(throws himself on the ground in a huge fit of temper)* WELL, I THOUGHT IT WAS FUNNY! I had a good time with Uncle Arthur and now I don't have a daddy, anymore. All the kids at school are going to ask me where my new daddy went to. They're going to think I made him up. They already think I made you up. And if you go away again, they'll know I made you up! *(bursts into tears)*

MOO	Stop snivelling. I'm not going away.
DOUGALL	Jane says my old Daddy sends you postcards and you go off to meet him. Why can't I meet him, too?
MOO	Jane is a spiteful little brat and she's dead wrong. I used to get postcards from your father but I told him not to send them, anymore. I travel because I enjoy travelling.
DOUGALL	Then why can't I come with you?
MOO	You have school.
DOUGALL	You just don't want me to come. *(pulls out postcard)* Here! Take it!
MOO	*(grabs postcard)* Oh, Dougall.
DOUGALL	It came in the mail, today.
MOO	*(reads)* Novo Rodondo. *(looks at DOUGALL)* I could try and bring him back.
DOUGALL	I know why you go.
MOO	Dougall?
DOUGALL	Go on! Go! You two play your stupid little game! See if I care! *(storms out)*

Act Two, Scene Fourteen

> MOO *and* DOUGALL. *He, aged sixteen, enters in army uniform.*

DOUGALL   How do I look?

MOO   Dreadful. I hate uniforms.

DOUGALL   I think I look pretty good.

MOO   You're too young. You're only sixteen.

DOUGALL   I'm in and there's nothing you can do about it. This time, I'll get to see the world.

MOO   It's a pretty stupid way to go about it. It's not a pleasure cruise, Dougall. It's a war. You could get killed.

DOUGALL   Would that disturb you?

MOO   God, how melodramatic you are. It's really very tiresome.

DOUGALL   That's me. Ever present and tiresome.

MOO   Please don't try to be cynical, Dougall. It's unbecoming.

DOUGALL   You never take me seriously, do you. I simply don't exist for you. Well, I'm remedying the situation. I, too, am vanishing out of your life. *(laughs)* I'll send you a postcard.

MOO   What!

DOUGALL   I'll find him for you, Mother. Don't
               worry. We'll both write. Two postcards.
               A matching set! *(leaves)*

MOO   Dougall? DOUGALL!

Act Two, Scene Fifteen

MOO, *in nursing home.*

MOO   The facts of life. I'm old and Harry
           Parker never loved me. I have done selfish
           things in my time, but I did them all out of
           a certain conviction that everything would
           come together. My youth and my love —
           foolish, frail, self-deceits. I wallow in
           them. And my son. No point even
           thinking about him. No point even
           thinking about anything. I'm an old dog
           left out in the rain. No one likes my smell
           and it's time to die.

Act Two, Scene Sixteen

*Nursing home. MOO'S room.
SUSAN enters tentatively. She is
carrying some presents.*

SUSAN	Hello, Aunt Moo.
MOO	Who are you?
SUSAN	Susan.
MOO	Susan.
SUSAN	Susan. Your niece. You and I were going to move to Samoa.
MOO	I'm sorry. I don't remember you.
SUSAN	I brought you Christmas presents.
MOO	Oh. Is it Christmas already?
SUSAN	It will be. Next week. You haven't really forgotten me, have you, Aunt Moo? I know you got mad at me for not going to Samoa but I couldn't just then. I had to finish Grade 11. I know you haven't forgotten. You're just pretending. All the relatives say you're senile but I know you're not. Don't worry. I'll get you out of here. You've been shut up too long. That's all. Your hip's all better so I don't know why they're keeping you here. Do you want to escape?
MOO	Who are you?

SUSAN   I'll help you escape. What do you need?
             Ropes? A file?

MOO   Gin.

SUSAN   You shouldn't drink, Aunt Moo.

MOO   Gin. I want gin.

SUSAN   Here's your presents. *(hands them to her)*

MOO   Is there gin?

SUSAN   I don't think so.

MOO   *(takes present and sings)* Happy Birthday
             to me...

SUSAN   It's Christmas, Aunt Moo.

MOO   *(continues)* Happy Birthday to me, Happy
             Birthday to Moragh, Happy Birthday to
             me. *(opens present)* My Sin. My
             favourite perfume, you know. It suits me.
             One should always have a perfume that
             suits one. An essence to leave behind.
             Men hate perfume. But I wear it, anyway.
             It tells them where I am. I used to wear
             this perfume as a joke. Of course, I liked
             the fragrance, but it was a joke. A sly
             joke. It backfired. I should have worn
             Joy. It would have been smarter to have
             worn Joy.

             Pause.

SUSAN   I'm studying anthropology, Aunt Moo.

MOO   What?

SUSAN   You remember. We talked about it, before. I have to ask you something.

MOO   Do you know those Chinese watercolour paintings? You know, the pretty pale ones with the little bird sitting on the jasmine branch —

SUSAN   This is important, Aunt Moo. I can't tell my mother. She'd have an absolute fit.

MOO   Whenever I see one of those paintings, with that tiny little bird sitting on the branch, do you know what I want to do? I want to take out my gun and shoot it! Blast its little brains out! *(bursts out laughing)* Isn't that awful?

SUSAN   Are you all right, Aunt Moo?

MOO   Of course, I'm just fine.

SUSAN   I have to tell you because you'd understand —

MOO   What perfume do you wear?

SUSAN   I don't wear perfume. You see —

MOO   How old are you?

SUSAN   Twenty.

MOO   Only twenty. You have your whole life ahead of you. *(laughs)*

Act Two, Scene Seventeen

SUSAN, *alone on stage.*

SUSAN | Of course, he doesn't love his wife. She means nothing to him. Well, he hasn't exactly told me that. Not in so many words. But, I can tell. I know he doesn't love her. I suppose it's in little things he does. The way he refers to her. As though she were an appendage. "Smith and I went down to the beach the other day. Of course, Smith likes all that stuff." He calls her "Smith", her maiden name. They went to school together and they used to call each other by their last names. He probably calls her "honey" when they're alone. Or "dear" so, I'm not ruining a wonderful marriage. It's not as though they have something great going together. It's the pits. They have a perfectly lousy relationship. He's just used to her. That's all. She's like the weather. It's only a matter of time before he leaves her. It's just a matter of time.

Act Two, Scene Eighteen

SUSAN *and* JANE.

SUSAN	I'm not going.
JANE	*(holds out presents)* It'll only take a minute, dear.
SUSAN	I'm not going. Why do I always have to give her the presents? I go every year and she doesn't even remember me.
JANE	She doesn't remember anyone, dear.
SUSAN	She'd remember you, Mother.
JANE	Would you please just do this for me?
SUSAN	She hates the perfume, Mother.
JANE	Oh. It used to be her favourite.
SUSAN	Well, she hates it now.
JANE	Should I give her something else?
SUSAN	No. I think she's gotten used to hating it.
JANE	Please do this for me. She's had a very unhappy life.
SUSAN	You always say that, Mother. Do you really think that just because a man leaves you it should ruin your life.

JANE   Her son left her, too. And I think both of them disappear —

SUSAN   Her son.

JANE   Yes. Dougall.

SUSAN   She had a son?

JANE   Yes. He disappeared during the war.

SUSAN   She never told me she had a son. Why didn't she talk about him?

JANE   *(matter-of-fact)* She never liked him much. But I'm sure she missed him. Once he was gone. I don't think he ran away. She was cruel to him but he never seemed to mind. I don't think he even noticed it. She was his mother, after all.

SUSAN   Mother, are you all right?

JANE   Yes. Yes, I'm all right,

SUSAN   Were you in love with him?

JANE   I loved him. Yes.

SUSAN   Did you have a love affair?

JANE   No. I just loved him. That's all.

SUSAN   Don't worry, Mother. I'll take the present to her.

JANE   Thank you, dear.

SUSAN   I'll take it every year from now on.

JANE   Thank you, dear.

Act Two, Scene Nineteen

Nursing home. MOO'S *room.*

SUSAN	*(enters with presents)* Merry Christmas, Aunt Moo.
MOO	Who are you?
SUSAN	Susan.
MOO	Do I know you?
SUSAN	You used to.
MOO	Sorry. I don't remember.
SUSAN	How about your son. Do you remember him?
MOO	*(muses)* My son.
SUSAN	We used to have long talks together. You and I. But you never mentioned your son. That was supposedly when you weren't senile. You had no excuse, then.
MOO	I'm old and I'm tired. I'm sorry. I don't understand what you're saying.
SUSAN	Why didn't you ever tell me about your son?
MOO	*(points to presents)* Those are presents, aren't they? Are they for me?

SUSAN   I'd like to talk about your son. I don't
               want to talk about your presents, women's
               rights, female oppression, your fucking
               "topics". I want to know what you did to
               your son.

MOO   See this. *(rolls up sleeve)* The nurses did
               this to me.

SUSAN   *(grabs her and shakes her)* What about
               your son!

MOO   See, there's a bruise. Look at my bruise.

SUSAN   You're pathetic. You know that. You're
               absolutely pathetic. I'm not going to wind
               up like you. Rambling. Senile. All those
               years and you didn't even mention his
               name.

MOO   All I wanted was some cigs and they
               wouldn't let me have them.

SUSAN   We're different, you know. I'm not like
               you.

MOO   Do you have any cigs? *(starts to paw*
               SUSAN *for cigs)*

SUSAN   You're fucking feeble-minded and it's all
               because of some man.

MOO   They tried to take my lighter away from
               me but I wouldn't let them have it.

SUSAN   I know what I want and I'm going after it.

MOO   The nurses grabbed me and they pinched me *(grabs* SUSAN'S *arm)* so I'd let go of the lighter. But I didn't let go.

SUSAN   *(grabs* MOO *and shakes her)* And I'm not letting go.

MOO   They pinched my arm but I didn't let go.

SUSAN   *(still shaking her)* I'm not letting go of you. You selfish old cow!

MOO   OW! OOOOOOOWW!! NURSE! NURSE! HELP ME NURSE!!!!

ORDERLY   *(enters)* Miss Parker —

MOO   *(shakily, pointing to* SUSAN) This woman —

SUSAN   I'm sorry. I gave her the presents and she attacked me.

ORDERLY   Yes. She's been doing that a lot lately. You know how it is. The mind goes and they're just like children again.

SUSAN   Yes. I understand.

MOO   *(holds out arm to* ORDERLY) My bruise.

Act Two, Scene Twenty

> *Nursing home.* HARRY *and* PATSY *enter.* MOO *is sitting in a chair nearby.* HARRY *sees* MOO, *stares at her.*

PATSY   I couldn't keep an eye on her all the time. And I mean she couldn't live with us.

HARRY   Mmmmmm.

PATSY   Are you all right?

HARRY   Yeah.

PATSY   It's sweet you're getting so depressed about my mother.

HARRY   Yeah.

PATSY   Honey, do you mind waiting here. I just want to go back and make sure she's okay. It might be a bit of a shock for her. You don't mind, do you?

HARRY   Hurry.

PATSY   You're a doll. *(leaves)*

MOO   *(looks up, sees* HARRY*)* Do you have a cig?

HARRY   No.

MOO   Oh.

        Pause.

MOO   *(rolls up sleeve)* See this. The nurses did this to me. I wanted some cigs but the nurses wouldn't let me have them. I found some though but they tried to take them away from me. But I wouldn't let go.

HARRY   I'm sure they didn't mean to.

MOO   Yes. They did. They grabbed me and tried to pinch me till I let go. Like this. *(grabs* HARRY'S *arm and pinches him)*

HARRY   OW!

MOO   They kept pinching and pinching but I wouldn't let go.

HARRY   Let go of me!

MOO   I held on and I wouldn't let go.

HARRY   Get the hell off me. *(throw her off his arm)*

MOO   They got my lighter, though. But they didn't get my cigs.

HARRY   Christ. What's happened to you. You're an old woman.

MOO   *(looks at him)* You're an old man.

HARRY   I guess I am. You don't remember, do you?

MOO   I could really use a cig.

HARRY   Here. *(hands her one)*

MOO   Thanks. Don't let the nurses know.

HARRY   No. I won't.

MOO   Do you have a light?

                       HARRY *lights it for her.*

PATSY   *(enters)* Sorry to take so long, dear. She's
                       a bit upset. They gave her some sedatives
                       so she should be all right.

HARRY   Let's go. *(starts to leave)*

MOO   Harry, HARRY!!

PATSY   That woman is pointing at you, dear. Do
                       you know her?

HARRY   I lit her cigarette.

MOO   HARRY!!

PATSY   She knows your name.

HARRY   Coincidence. Come on, let's get out of
                       here.

                       HARRY *rushes* **PATSY** *out.*

MOO   Harry. Are you going to send me a
                       postcard? Do you have a postcard for me,
                       Harry? Do you have a postcard?

Act Two, Scene Twenty-one

> *Nursing home. MOO's room.*
> *Darkness. MOO is in bed, asleep.*

HARRY   *(opens door)* Moo? *(goes to MOO, takes her hand)* What beautiful hands you have. You always had beautiful hands.

MOO   *(wakes up)* Harry?

HARRY   *(pulls out a small handgun, places MOO's hand on gun)* Yes, Moo. It's me. *(raises gun to MOO'S heart)*

> MOO *does not resist. She and* HARRY *pull the trigger. The gun goes off quietly. He leaves by the window.*

Act Two, Scene Twenty-two

HARRY *and* PATSY *in front of the television set.*

PATSY   Are you happy with me, Harry?

HARRY   Of course, Patsy.

PATSY   Really happy?

HARRY   Yes.

PATSY   You wouldn't rather be somewhere else.

HARRY   No. Not right now.

PATSY   I thought you always wanted to live on a desert island.

HARRY   I did.

PATSY   Do you still want to?

HARRY   Patsy, life with you is a desert island.

PATSY   Harry.

The End